"In *The Longing*, Paul Hooker bids us to follow his journey, a pilgrimage where surprises continue to create tension and discovery that lead to certainty and questioning. His poetry evokes a sense of anticipation, curiosity, and wonder, priming the reader to engage with immediate feelings spurred by irony, nostalgia, certainty, and more in the poetry. Here we discover that it is longing that connects us, and longing is the journey we embark upon as creation and Creator."

—ASHLEY R. SANDERS, pastor, Presbyterian Church on Edisto Island

"To borrow Paul Hooker's verb, the Holy 'peeks' through the words, the silences, the lines of both the poems and the prose on these pages. To read this book is to embark on a pilgrimage whose end will return you, dust to dust, to the beginning, as one whose longing has been deepened, enlarged, amazed."

—CYNTHIA JARVIS, pastor emerita, Presbyterian Church of Chestnut Hill

"Paul Hooker's *The Longing* offers an arc of meditations on absence that is somehow presence, or its inverse, which in Hooker's writing blurs into the same thing. Blurred, too, are any lines between divine and earthly, of holy and not. What do you know of these things? Hooker challenges the reader to take what they think they know, and think they don't, and look again."

—KIMBOL SOQUES, poet and theopoetics scholar

"The poems of *The Longing* are the work of a mind partly wizened. Withered are certainties and naivetes familiar to people, like Hooker, of Christian faith and church. What endures are erudition, mental alacrity, creativity. Newborn is honest embrace of ambiguity, and suspicion that no signifier is more ambiguous than 'God.' The effect is typically unsettling, at times disturbing, but consistently provocative, evocative, and productive."

—WILLIAM GREENWAY, professor of philosophical theology, Austin Presbyterian Theological Seminary

THE LONGING

THE LONGING

Poems

Paul K. Hooker

RESOURCE *Publications* • Eugene, Oregon

THE LONGING
Poems

Resource Publications
An Imprint of Wipf and Stock Publishers
199 W. 8th Ave., Suite 3
Eugene, OR 97401

www.wipfandstock.com

PAPERBACK ISBN: 979-8-3852-1178-4
HARDCOVER ISBN: 979-8-3852-1179-1
EBOOK ISBN: 979-8-3852-1180-7

03/27/24

Si enim comprehendis, non est Deus

—Augustine of Hippo, Sermon 117

Contents

Contents

Contents

SIGHTINGS OF THE HOLY

Preface

A poet has no right to dictate what a poem means. What a reader takes from a poem is a right belonging exclusively to the reader. But perhaps a poet may be permitted to say why a poem distilled itself into language and precipitated on the page.

In the case of the present poems, I can say that they are the result of some years of longing. I haven't always known I felt a longing. For some time I misread longing as impatience or petulance, irritation, dissatisfaction, even dread. I was aware that, in various corners of my consciousness, there were these ill-named feelings, along with a sense that something was missing that once was there, something I hadn't known I needed to know. Something for which I had no name.

Then some years ago, I began reading the mystics—theologians and philosophers from the second century CE onward who share in various ways a starting place in neo-Platonism. Their names are well known to historians of spirituality: Proclus, Plotinus, Gregory of Nyssa, Pseudo-Dionysius the Areopagite, Teresa of Avila, Julian of Norwich, the anonymous author of *The Cloud of Unknowing*, Meister Eckhart, Marguerite Porete, San Juan de la Cruz, Nicholas of Cusa, the Kabbalists Moses ben Cordovero and Isaac Luria, the Sufi Ibn al-'Arabi. And modern writers, too, philosophers and poets: Annie Dillard, Belden Lane, Emmanuel Levinas, Gerard Manley Hopkins, Rainer Maria Rilke, Wallace Stevens, Jean-Luc Marion, Paul Ricoeur, Pierre Teilhard de Chardin. I make no claim to plumb the depths of what any of these shining souls have said. But something of what they sought gives shape and substance to the something I have been seeking.

I am a Christian, a Presbyterian minister by training and lifelong practice. For most of my life, the word "God" has slipped comfortably from the rear of my palate to the tip of my tongue at the back of my teeth and out into the world of pious and professional conversation. But one of the results of my mystical journey has been a reticence to name the One Who Has No Name. I have grown more and more uncomfortable with—indeed, repulsed by—the assumption made by many with whom I share faith community that "God" is knowable, personal, or relational. So strong is this revulsion that I have stopped using the term altogether. I use a variety of nouns—the One, the Infinite, the Holy, all of which as devoid of projected personality as I can make them—to describe an Ultimate Reality that remains not only indescribable but unknowable and unsayable. At the heart of my longing has been a yearning for what I will not and cannot have: an encounter with that Something. Indeed, I long for but do not possess an adequate language with which to render that Something. At best, I think, the poet (or at least this poet) can only finally peer into the darkness and try to limn the shape of what once was there.

Perhaps the best metaphor for that missing Something is the image in Genesis 3:24 of Adam and Eve, now expelled from Eden, their return to Paradise now barred by the ever-turning *lahat-hahereb* ("sword of flame"). At least to my imagination, no other image quite as well captures the sense of having had Something once . . . and lost it. I find myself wondering, whenever I venture into an occasion of Christian worship, whether the congregation is even aware that we once had Something, and that we have lost it, and that we will never get it back, and that the vague sense of ache and illness-at-ease we feel is the longing for the missing Something. Is a missing Something still Something? Or has it become Nothing, an absence, an emptiness?

But I wonder, too, whether that Nothing, that emptiness, lurks behind and beneath so many of the stories that make up the Judeo-Christian scriptural tradition. I read the narratives that comprise the sacred texts of my tradition with the sense that they point never so much to the presence of Something as to its absence, to a *deus absconditus* always escaping our sight and eluding our grasp.

And I wonder whether that Nothing, that emptiness, makes its appearance in other forms and more narrowly defined places. The struggle for emotional and sexual intimacy, and the memory of love lost to the ravages of time and the vicissitudes of fortune. The approach of the end of a career, and the inevitable awareness that all one's achievements will pass from mind no sooner than the office lights are turned off and the office door is for a final time closed and locked. Advancing age, and the approach of death. There is, it seems to me, a longing writ deep in each of these experiences.

Finally, I wonder whether that Nothing, while it never reveals itself, also never allows us to stop seeking it. Like a dust-devil in the desert, like a mirage shimmering on the horizon, it promises that which it will never deliver and compels us toward a destination at which we will never arrive. And yet, my everyday experience of the world bears out the truth of Hopkins's exclamation, that the Holy "over the bent/world broods with warm breast and with ah! bright wings."[1] The shining pinions of Hopkins's Spirit lure me ever onward down the darkened path of believing, illumining the next step if not the journey whole.

❖ ❖ ❖

There are people without whose minds, hearts, words, and faith in me these poems would not have been written. My colleagues on the faculty of Austin Presbyterian Theological Seminary, where I taught for ten years, read these poems, posed questions, challenged assumptions, and sharpened my language. Especially, I am grateful to Cynthia Rigby, whose brilliant theological mind is always dancing at the edges of the known; to William Greenway, whose equally brilliant mind is paralleled only by his skill as an editor, and who contributed significantly to the quality of the

1. Gerard Manley Hopkins, "God's Grandeur," *Gerard Manley Hopkins: Poems and Prose*. Penguin Press, 1985.

essay that closes this book; to Lewis Donelson, himself a poet of no mean skill and a reader of great gentleness and sensitivity; to David Johnson, whose facility with the medieval apophatic tradition opened doors of awareness that are of immense value to me, and whose patient yet persistent questions sharpened my understanding of my own words; and to David White, a scholar of both Christian spiritual practice and theological aesthetics, with whom I shared the various drafts of this work and who over innumerable lunches of Korean food gave me both wise critique and a bolstered courage. I must also thank students in classes on poetry and theology in both the Master of Divinity and Doctor of Ministry curricula at the seminary, who read and reacted to poems in this book, and especially to Kimbol Soques, former student, friend, and fellow poet, whose encouragement and clear-eyed readings of these poems were indispensable in their formation. Finally, I must thank my wife and partner in life, Patricia Thiede, without whose love the sun would not rise in the morning and in whose presence the Holy is most reliably visible to me.

PAUL HOOKER
January 2024

THE LONGING

I

The Cave

Beauty is the name of what we have lost. And what we have lost makes itself present as longing and desire.

—Rubem A. Alves, *The Poet, the Warrior, the Prophet*

BEGINNINGS

In the cave-dark
of my childhood
I sensed it beside me
once.

In the darkening
penult of my days
will it be there
once again?

THE ROCK IN THE DARKNESS

Cumberland Caverns, 1965

I remember mud
caked on sneakers (not my good ones, mind you,
but good enough to make my mother mad)
and slathered like noxious icing
up to the knees of my blue jeans
(sure prompt to yet greater maternal ire).

Slithering like salamanders
between ancient rocks, a needle's-eye
adventure for a boy descending
with each passage farther from his moorings,
leaving the familiar ease of sunlight
for a sortie in the bowels the earth.

Brownish-yellow lights
strung like ill-used Christmas ornaments,
covered now in cave-dust, ground
from stones that can recall no sunlight.
They limned the sloping path deeper, farther
from the fading, dwindling hope of day.

Subterranean chamber
half a mile down in the gathering murk:
we filtered in, like dust motes rising from
the winding sheet that shrouded every rock,
dust that once *was* every rock, now
pulverized by the pressures of the world.

Sitting down as I was told
(obedient child!) beside the chamber wall
that was no wall, but only the nearest cheekbone
of the craggy visage of creation,
as though the world above me was a stylite,
and I sat near the footing of its plinth.

Dust—the acrid smell
pungent in my nose—the dust of death
to which all life goes down, until
it finds its last repose on rocky crags
in this cavern-casket. Whose life had I
dislodged with my finger's idle graze?

Afraid of the dark?
someone asked, hand resting on the terminal,
another father's son, but unlike me,
accustomed to the dark, or so it seemed.
No flashlights, came the word, and then
the light of the world went out.

We count on light,
even in the darkness, some *reshimu* left
when the Light withdraws, goes wherever
light goes when darkness falls. Always
some half-lit shadow, some half-hope of day,
some echo of a star, some faded moon.

But not that night,
not in that chambered sarcophagus.
Such Darkness never fell with setting sun,

that yet sustains the memory of Light
and the hope of a tomorrow, not with kindness
born of gentle twilights past,

but ferocious,
Yeats's rough beast sprung from silent ambush,
malevolent maw of chaos dragon yawning,
swallowing creation, past beak to gizzard
where cave-grit grinds convenient comforts
into blackening cloud, anonymous and cold.

I had been a boy,
a son, a brother, sixth grader who played baseball
and read books about Indian chiefs.
That child leaked into the ravening dark,
dissolving into the cloud, atom by atom.
I heard the sound of my own voice screaming.

Gone the chamber floor,
the acrid dust no longer on the stones
but swirling, pitching, yawing, hapless spirits
spinning in the void—no up or down,
no right or left, no good or wrong. No truth.
In the Dark, true and false are one.

Falling, rolling, gone—
I am become a roiling dust devil
dispersing in the howling windswept Dark,
molecules once honored with a name
no one could any more recall.
Balance, gravity, identity—all gone.

Only one shred left:
pure instinct. A hand outstretched
to catch its erstwhile body in mid-stumble—
not my hand, for I was not, but like a hand
still connected with something like a brain—
a hand reached out . . .

       . . . and touched the Rock.
Not *a* rock, a thing so small, so common,
so *known* and normal as might be skipped
across a pond or dug up from a creek-bed
to expose a crawdad for a day's delight
in a distant, dissociated dream of childhood.

A hand reached out . . .
and touched the One, the deep-sunk piling,
rooted in creation's basement, there to bear
burden of the world. I touched the Rock.
And the dust precipitated in the darkling cloud,
became my form, and I was myself again,

a boy, a son, a brother,
sixth grader on a camping trip inside a cave,
whose mother would spare not her wrath
at the ruination of his slacks and sneakers.
Brownish-yellow lights flickered on
and the world came home. Only,

something was different
(though it would be years before I understood).
Before the lights went out, had you asked

what I believed in, I would have said
God and Jesus, home and school,
baseball and books about Indian chiefs.

When light returned,
I trusted none of these, nor have I since.
Such skittish truths as these are little more
than footlights, brownish-yellow bulbs
caked with the dust of lives lived in their glow,
they light the step, but not the journey whole.

I believe in the One,
Silent in the void, unseen, unsaid,
unknown Ground-stone in the tumbling Dark,
beyond all being, it has no name
responds to no summons, obeys no law.
I believe in the Rock in the Darkness.

The Rock is still there. It dwells unseen,
in the Darkness in the basement of creation.
When the lights go out, I reach out a hand
and hope again to touch it. In the Dark,
all things are one thing, and the one thing is the One.
I am reaching still.

II

Love in the Sand

If two lie together, they keep warm; but how can one keep warm alone?

—ECCLESIASTES 4:11

COUPLES

A bed
is an ocean
in the darkness where

lovers
sail past each other
just out of hailing distance.

OVERDOSE: A MINOR BALLAD

Brumbly Bob and the sweet BittyBoo
tussled all day with the toodle-dee-doo.
They weren't yet one but no longer two.
And the longing was all that either one knew.

They hummeled and bummeled with all of their might;
'twas the best they could do in the stars' frosty light.
They were never quite wrong and never quite right
as they lay on the sand in the dark of the night.

Said Bob to the 'Boo: "I think I have found
a way we can fly with our feet on the ground.
It's love in a bottle, the best stuff around,"
as his words washed away in the dark waves and drowned.

"Here in my hand, by the light of the moon,
is a serving of bliss in the bowl of a spoon.
If we aren't too late and we aren't too soon
we'll mix up some magic in the lee of the dune."

Said the 'Boo in a while: "I'm floating on air
with the stars in my eyes and the wind in my hair.
I'm not really here, and I'm not really there.
If I never come down, will anyone care?"

It's hard to predict what meanings emerge
when you fall through the fog and land on the verge.
It's partly fandango and partly a dirge
that the dark waves dance in the green ocean surge.

Uniformed eyes make routine observations.
The obvious doesn't require explanation.
They neither confirm nor deny allegations,
but pack up their kits and go back to the station.

The waves swell and, cresting, return to their bed
in the sea, never resting but swelling instead.
It's never quite secret and never quite said,
but the living make room for the still-longing dead.

Did Brumbly Bob and the sweet BittyBoo
finally master the toodle-dee-doo?
I haven't an answer, and neither have you.
But the stars and the sand know. The ocean knows, too.

WAVES[1]

The past is the present experienced as longing.
—RUBEM ALVES, THE POET, THE WARRIOR, THE PROPHET

At night the old man comes back to the waves
    swelling, sparkling in the moonlight,
        failing, falling back to swell again.
They never reach his bench
    safe and dry
        on the high side of the berm.
He yearns for a morning when
    he returns home
        with wet shoes.

1. This poem first appeared on 27 July 2023 at PoetryBreakfast.com.

She is with him—
    something stirring deep inside
        rising from the aquifers of heartache,
swelling, surging, a freshening breeze:
    moist breath on his lips before her kiss
        fragrant hair feathering his face
the weight of her breast
    in the trembling palm
        of his hand.

The sand is their dominion;
    the night sky keeps its watch
        and stars are footlights all along their way.
They are each other's still-untrodden path
    a way of wonders in the shining darkness.
        Each the invitation to the other's feast.
He puts out his hand, reaching for
    the fruit he has tasted in his dreams
        forbidden everywhere but here . . .

and she evanesces in the darkness.
    The wind turns cold.
        Storm clouds gather somewhere out to sea.

He wonders: is memory but exuvia,
    Cenotaph to a firefly
        long since gone to wing?
Meanwhile, the waves with each swell bring ashore
    a present sparkling with its tidal past.
        The morning marks moist footprints on the sand.

III

Library

Of making many books there is no end, and much study is a weariness of the flesh.
—ECCLESIASTES 12:12

LEAVING

The hand that
turns off the light

may not be

the hand that
closes the door.

ESTIMATE OF WORTH

These books that cost a fortune in their day
are worth a pittance now to current eyes,
and I shall have to let them blow away.

Boxed and carted out in sad array—
a one-man job; none else to sympathize.
These books cost me a fortune in their day.

Their bindings tell what I am loathe to say,
what knowledge of their contents testifies:
ephemeral, they all must blow away.

So many years of words. Did they convey
what now I've hardly breath to analyze?
These books that cost a fortune in their day

were little more than passing fancy, play
of sound or ink or thought. They atomize.
Naught else to do but let them blow away.

Knowing is like breathing in its way:
the one who tries to hold his breath will die.
And what once cost a fortune in its day
like dust will lastly all be blown away.

IV

Liturgy

Guard your steps when you go into the house of God; to draw near to listen is better than the sacrifice of fools.

—ECCLESIASTES 5:1

CALL TO WORSHIP

Our help is in the One by whom
all heaven and earth was made,
whose name, unknown, once filled this room,
who heard all prayers, unprayed,
but now is gone. An empty tomb.
And yet we come, afraid
of sharp regrets within the gloom,
of debts as yet unpaid.
We dare not hope nor speak too soon
lest, welcome overstayed,
we're swept to realms inopportune
where life's in balance weighed.
And so begins our mummery
to gods of gentler memory.

Nothing happens in this room.
That is why we come.

GATHERING PRAYER

O You before whom hidden things are plain,
our secret wants, our paltry fears laid bare,
we in this sacred hour to you repair.
O cleanse, we pray, our minds of earthly stain.
Banish any thought that might constrain
the heart's devotion. In this rarer air
we come to lose the clinging weight we bear,
to gain release, to praise your holy name.
And for whatever fears our hearts retain
we seek forgiveness in advance, for cares
we cannot shake, must carry everywhere,
even here, which renders effort vain
to sing the angels' anthem. To that end
we pray through Christ our Lord, and say **Amen.**

The pews creak beneath the burden
not just of bodies dressed in coats and suits,
nor harried mothers, fathers, squirmy children,
but of careworn spirits, sour fruit
of nights spent sleepless, tossing, turning
with some formless, non-specific yearning
we carried in the door. It has no name
but gathers like a storm-cloud before a rain.

CONFESSION OF SIN

Merciful Savior, we confess
we've gathered under some duress

from forces we don't comprehend,
that overwhelm us in the end.
We're loathe to own the sinner's claim:
that we're at fault, that we're to blame.
We generalize, and stall and shill,
and slip the noose. Or better still,
we throw ourselves at Mercy's seat
and hope mere justice finds defeat
in pardon, though we rate the rod.
Such is our prayer, sweet Mercy's God.

> We walk in holy canyons before a rain,
> before the drowning torrent washes clean
> the remnants of unsanctified terrain.
> Listen! Rumblings of the storm as yet unseen.
> This is the honest hour, when all pretense has flown.
> Nothing knows, and Nothing is unknown.

PARDON

The costly mercy of the Lord,
we tell ourselves, is freely given,
and thus take heart to hear this word:
Your sin, though grave, has all been shriven.

> What does forgiveness cost?
> Not blood, and not vicarious death,
> not fealty to the dead, whose hope is lost,
> nor to the living, we who hold our breath
> against our guilt. No, the cost is sight:
> something we saw once before, now gone,
> fled before the fall of darkling night.
> But the shape of it—of Nothing—lingers on.

THE WORD: A PRAYER FOR ILLUMINATION

O Word, turn the soil of hardened minds
with the Spirit's harrow. Inseminate
these new-cut furrows plowed and left behind
with seeds of promise flung out profligate.
Spirit, speak your word to this your Church,
and soothe at last our heartsore, lonely search.

> *The angel wields a sword to bar the way*
> *to Nothing, and to hope. Nonetheless*
> *the heart's eye sees what time has swept away:*
> *vestiges of grace. We confess*
> *a dim and distant longing, scarce concealed,*
> *like friends who once were lovers sometimes feel.*

EUCHARIST

On the night in which he was betrayed
he took the loaf and giving up his thanks,
"Remember me," in quiet voice he said,
and broke and passed it down their ragged ranks.

He took the cup, poured out a generous draft,
and held it up for every eye to see
as I do now, with ancient priestly craft:
"When you drink of this, remember me."

Remember, then, that those who take this meal
sit not alone in porous memory's pew,
but with the saints into his presence real
are gathered by a Spirit hid from view.

Such love in loaf and chalice, held aloft:
The shape of what we had, and what we've lost.

> *Holy words said, holy music sung,*
> *holy food set out in holy ware.*
> *Nothing makes them holy and makes us one.*
> *And Nothing at the last will meet us where*
> *the shape of Nothing rises from the table*
> *and greets us there, as willing eyes are able.*

PASTORAL PRAYER

[Pardon, please, this minor fit of spleen.
Every week I stand here in this spot
with table, laid with holy ware, between
me and them and, while I'd rather not,
I recite the latest catalogue
of chaos, natural and human-made:
California fires and Chinese smog,
invasions, school shootings—the hit parade
of mayhem. The same prayer every week.
You must get tired of plaintive cries, no less
Than I do of the silence of the meek.
All of which leads me to wonder this:
Are you listening? Is anyone at home?
Or am I merely standing here alone?]

> *Beyond the reach of prayers for grace, surpassing*
> *justice neither blind nor balanced true,*
> *solace trickles down in wordless blessing,*
> *like drops from canyon walls after a deluge,*
> *oblations to the One whom none can claim,*
> *who obeys no law and has no name.*

BENEDICTION

Go out into the world in peace
hold to what we pray is real:
a love that does not pause or cease
though you may never see nor feel
it there. Take now some little shred
of hope, some glimmer of the light
to shine along the paths of dread
and briefly tame the ravening night.
'Tis this light alone we raise.
Bless the Lord. **God's name be praised.**

Nothing happens in this room.
That is why we come.

V

Last Words

The end of the matter; all has been heard.
Fear God and keep his commandments;
for that is the whole duty of everyone.
—ECCLESIASTES 12:13

EYE TEST

How clear
one's vision

when looking
from the end.

THE TEACHER'S LAST ADVICE

(*a poetic translation of Ecclesiastes 12:1–7*)

Recall in days when you are young
the One who shaped your frame
before the hard times steal desire,
and years erase your name,

before the sun, the moon, the stars
all darken like the night,
and clouds once shed of rainfall
remain to shroud the light.

Too soon the house's guards grow weak,
the strong too frail to rise;
the few who grind the grain cease work,
and dim the watchers' eyes.

The doorways to the street, now closed,
mute the gristmill's noise,
allow a bird to stir your sleep
but silence music's voice.

Fear dwells in all the towering heights
and terrors in the road;
the almond tree blooms all in white,
the grasshopper drags his load,

and desire wilts. Then go at last
to life's last resting place,

while mourners weeping in the street
have all forgot your face.

But ere is cut life's silver cord
and smashed the golden urn,
and ewer shattered at the well
and wheel by cistern spurned,

and dust returned to dust and ash
and spirit whence it came,
recall the One who gave you life,
though you know not Its name.

SEVENTY

I said, "I am old." You said,
"Do not say that. You're not old."

You're right. Age is, as they say,
just a number, and seventy

is the new fifty. Or some such nonsense.
I have no idea what that means.

Here is what I mean: I mean to rid myself
of pretenses I have shouldered since my youth.

I mean to leave behind the selves
I have worn like someone else's clothes.

The Longing

I mean to give up dusting my bookshelves and leave
the sediment of knowing to settle where it will.

I mean to grope my way into the shining darkness.
I mean to climb like Moses up the clouded mountain.

Somewhere in each day, there is an old man.
He smiles and puts a finger to his lips,

reminds me that I should exhale perspicaciously,
that breathing is a finite, numbered rhythm,

and climbing mountains takes a lot of breath.
He's right, of course, and so are you.

Age is just a number. Like the number
of times I have exhaled while I wrote this poem.

VI

Homo et Deus Imperfectus

I have seen the busywork that God has given mortals to be busy with. He has made everything beautiful in its time, and yet he has put eternity into their minds, so that they cannot discover the doings of God from beginning to end.

—ECCLESIASTES 3:10–11 (AUTHOR'S TRANSLATION)

BERESHITH ("IN THE BEGINNING")

In the beginning, . . .

—GENESIS 1:1

In the beginning
was the One

And the One was All
and Nothing.

TSIMTSUM ("WITHDRAWAL")

The problem at the core is simply put:
if in the darkness there is only One
and if the One is One, is All in All,
and within the One is no distinction
or difference, dichotomy, or change,
what place is there within the One for anything

that is not the One, anything
that opens eyes and draws a breath and puts
its feet upon resistant ground, can change
its mind? If finally there is only One,
what meaning can there be within distinction?
Why create creation after all?

In the silence of the One, the One is All.
And Nothing. There is not anything
as interesting as difference or distinction,
no thing to pout, to shake its fist, to put
its foot down, shout "No" against the One,
demand of the Changeless that it change.

Does the One exchange serenity for change?
Does the One yearn for the many after all?
In the silent Oneness of the One
the first act's not the "let there be" of anything.
It is withdrawal, an emptiness to put
the many in, and difference, and distinction.

Tsimtsum. The birthing of distinction,
the opening door, the first moment of change.

26

The One gives up Itself, and there will put
all that is not Itself, cease to be All
in All, become a part of things, a *thing*,
longing now for what was once the One.

What does it mean to cease to be the One?
How deep within the One resides distinction?
This superflux of love that yearns for something
not now found in stillness, but in change
will never find completion. But in us all
it sets Desire, this restless longing, puts

anything and everything in motion, puts
change within our hearts, while the One
without distinction dwells within us all.

LAHAT-HAḤEREB ("THE FLAMING SWORD")

. . . and at the east of the garden of Eden he placed the cheru-bim, and a sword flaming and turning to guard the way to the tree of life.

—GENESIS 3:24

1.

Let us create them. Let them stand and see
what animals and angels cannot know,
that fruit of knowledge hangs from every tree,
not just that one of which I said: Here, no.
We grow them from the dust. So let them be

curious what fruit from dust may grow,
this soil of rebel soul and willful heart,
resident within them from the start.

Is there no end, you ask, to rebel claims?
How far from pure creation may they fall
before divine Desire forgets their names
and banishes them where gods cannot recall,
and bars return with wheeling sword of flame—
a barrier more stern than any wall?
I will not forget. Their heart is mine
and mine is theirs. Will they return in time?

Why, you ask? Do you not feel this fire
that surges even now within the breast,
this wild upwelling of divine Desire,
a single ray more brilliant than the rest
of all the stars, a ray that falls from higher
than mind can climb, than spirit can attest?
We make what makes us; they are fire undimmed.
Let them long for fire, as I for them.

Nor will this longing cease, nor slow its pace
within my heart. It is love's aftermath
that leaves an empty hole, a lover's place
beneath the sheets, an ache that outlasts wrath.
Diminish not this yearning, though darkened space
may hide from them this last illumined path.
Extinguish not this beacon! This, my final word.
Mark now this spot. I plant the flaming sword.

2.

Look! There's the sword. Rather, don't look back.
Best now to leave behind the things we've lost
and try to chase from mind the world we lack
and claim a new one, never mind the cost.
One foot before the other, up the track.
Trek the mountain pass and ford the floss.
Perhaps it's not the garden, pure and fine.
Still, we'll get accustomed, given time.

Which is not to say that all is well
or even good enough. What once was free
is now bought dear, as sweat alone can tell.
And what came easy once 'tween you and me
lies buried deep where only heartaches dwell.
This is, I guess, the way it has to be.
Still the longing keeps an empty space of pain
where you once lived, if never there again.

But something more. The longing is not done
when we have fumbled through our *pas-de-deux*,
and you're asleep, and I am left alone.
In the dark, it is as if I knew
a Light somewhere, a place deep in that bone
I sacrificed to be not one but two.
Desire lived there, was pure and whole and free,
before the sword . . . but I no longer see.

Is longing but the shape of lost Desire?
Is yearning but the sign of ceaseless change,
a smothered flame, all that's left of fire

that once burned wild, but now is tamed
in dust and ash, as mortal life requires,
banked and waiting still to yield its flame?
It smolders yet, and will until we die—
is not put out, no matter how we try.

VII

The Canyon

Standing naked before the divine resplendence, they discover the indifference of God to be yet another form of God's insistent love.

—BELDEN LANE, *THE SOLACE OF FIERCE LANDSCAPES*

TABLE

No meat so rich, no wine so strong,
no table bought so dear

as this before you laid: the feast
of One who is not here.

PLAZA BLANCA

I am climbing, slowly.
The path is on a slight incline, threaded
between canyon walls. Sandstone columns,
crisp and razor-edged, cut the cerulean sky
like a scalpel slicing through pericardium
searching for a soul.

I am in search of Nothing.
High in north New Mexico, in an arroyo,
I saw it once, some years ago, a wisp
of dust (I think?) drifting round the path's next turn,
and for a moment I was Moses, face hid
in the cleft of rock.

Does the One still haunt the clouded mountain?
A rattlesnake coils, sunning on the ledge,
acknowledging with flicking tongue the dust
my boots have stirred. Clouds gather in the west.
The coming storm will wash the canyon clean
of any last remains of me.

The trailhead was a celebration:
hoodoos circling 'round a central column,
giant *jaliscienses,* frozen in sandstone,
dancing an eternal *jarabe tapatio*
with some elusive, unseen lover.
I don't know how to dance.

Walk up the path, between the walls
rising sixty feet into the air.

Pass the Cathedral: sandstone organ pipes
intone an alien mass upon the ear.
They make no effort to translate their liturgy.
All else is silence.

This is the temple of the Holy.
The One is here, has only now just vanished
up ahead where the trail turns through a gap.
I will not see. The Holy is not for my eyes
to capture, nor feeble minds like mine
to comprehend.

Wait! There! Is that the robe hem of the Holy,
evanescent vision in the desert sun,
or only vestige of a dust devil twirling
in its own ethereal dance, a momentary whiff
of rarefaction, the One reduced to ephemera
in the superheated air?

But climb on, the rocks beckon and compel.
The trail narrows, and the walls lean in
as if to whisper *sic transit* in my ears,
as though I might not recall that I
like all things am but passing through this place
and must soon die.

I come at last to trail's end, a crevice
where eternal wall conjoins eternal wall.
No hand-made ladder will reach the Holy's dreams.
Here pilgrims are denied their journey's goal.

Here ancient sailors sail off the edge of maps.
Here indeed are dragons.

This is the kingdom of the One
known only by unknowing and unsaying,
whose angels are rattlesnakes, whose word is silence,
whose grace pours down from thunderclouds
and rages unrestrained through canyon walls
in deadly, life-filled torrents.

I must not overstay my welcome.
Yet I have returned, and will return again,
for there is no resisting, no other breath
that breathes this dust, no other blood that pulses
in my veins, nor heart that beats with mine
but that is here.

With crisp awareness or in vague compulsion,
we all long for this rock-strewn pilgrimage,
yearn to walk this pathway through this dust
with eyes alert for visions of the One
we will never see. And, unseeing, still we come,
because the Holy beckons.

Rise, then; approach in penitence,
while snakes and silent columns share their secret,
a darkling truth too deep for words
and older than creation, a knowing long forgot
in dust of death: Come, they say.
See, all things are ready.

The Holy bids: with open, outstretched hand
Reach out, and take, and eat
a morsel of my rocky splendor, drink
a draft of my indifferent dust, and know:
All things are one thing, and the one thing is the One.
We are reaching still.

TRADITIONS

JOSEPH'S BONES[1]

The bones of Joseph, which the Israelites had brought up from Egypt, were buried at Shechem, in the portion of the land Jacob had bought from the children of Hamor, the father of Shechem, for one hundred pieces of money; it became an inheritance of the descendants of Joseph.

—JOSHUA 24:32

Impossibly long the trail
up from parted water,
across the ancient sands,
through empty desolations
no one cares to own,
to a stopping place safe
from the whip, beneath a willow tree.
The earth is weeping;
each step a tear,
witness to the passing of his bones.

He is laid to rest—
if there is such a thing as rest
in this migrant life, always
moving with the rhythms of the world,
one step ahead of terror,
one step short of grace.
His father bought this land, they say.
He is at peace, they say.

1. Original publication in *The Presbyterian Outlook.*

It is inheritance, they say,
this land, this rock-hewn charnel for his bones.

But who belongs here? Who knows
any peace but the sweet caress
of the morning breeze, the fiery breath
of the mid-day sun, the cold rebuke
of the night-wind beneath the silent stars?
Lay claim to this dirt, even
at the cost of blood and bitter gall.
The deed may be in hand
but it will surely be contested,
and no defense be offered by the bones.

Others will inherit, too, in time,
when you have gone, scaled
another chain-link fence, waded
another muddy river, passed beneath
another scowling border guard
with rifle eager for a lucky shot.
Move on, move on, until the earth reveals
its pillow for your head,
its blanket for your chill,
its inheritance for your lonely bones.

AS ONE UNKNOWN

He comes to us as One unknown, without a name, as of old,
beside the lake. . ..

—ALBERT SCHWEITZER, THE QUEST FOR THE HISTORICAL JESUS

He comes to us.
We know his name.
It is the *cause célèbre* of the day—
we brook no opposition, are assured of
the purity of our own righteousness.
'Tis the hour of the advocate, the true believer.
We believe. No room for doubt.

He comes to us.
We know the question.
It is Pilate's query, writ anew:
What is justice? (Let alone, what truth?)
The answer on the lips is passion's howl.
The time for talk is done: the streets are ours.
We march. No time for waiting.

He comes to us.
We know the story.
It is the fantasy of resurrection:
a managed little death, and then tomorrow
stones roll aside and we emerge unscathed
to build proud towers that will touch the sky.
We own no king in "kin-dom."

He comes to us.
We do not recognize him.
He is the eternal watcher on the shore
beside the lake, his mystery unguessed,
while we flail the water with empty nets.
His kingdom is not here. He weeps because
he knows no life but dying.

JOSEPH ACQUIESCES TO HIS FATE

Her husband Joseph, being a righteous man and unwilling to
expose her to public disgrace, planned to dismiss her quietly.
—MATTHEW 2:19

I have a reputation to uphold.
Not that you would know, but in this town
I am looked up to, I am told,
the object of some praise, even renown.
This will not do, this girl whose belly holds
a child whose father's nowhere to be found.
I won't have scandal sniffing at my feet.
An end is what I need, quiet, discreet.

This is no time for children out of wed
whose lineage is prone to imprecision,
whose origin in some unmarried bed
provokes a man like me to hard decisions.
Still, I am fond of her, and in my head
I cannot bear the thought of her derision.
Let her go some other where, not here;
a clinic where such problems disappear.

Fear not, you say? Do you know what that means?
You angels have no fear of human law
designed to capture folk like us between
the cost of peace of mind and moral flaw.
Are surgical solutions so obscene

but carrying the child not the last straw?
You haunt my dreams and promise me salvation
but ignore the danger of the situation.

Yehoshua, you say, shall be the name
that echoes down the halls of history
and bears the hope of nations. But the blame
for off'ring hapless peasants just like me
false hope that one day hearts will change
will fall upon my shoulders. Wait and see.
You want my word? Then let thy will be done.
Joseph may have a child, but God a Son.

CHRISTMAS ROSE

Lo, how a Rose e'er blooming from tender stem hath sprung!
—Traditional German Carol

Were there roses before there were thorns?
Or did thorns give rise to roses?

Rilke said,
*Denn das Schöne ist nichts als des Schrecklichen Anfang. . .. ***

And Stevens,
"Death is the mother of beauty. . .."

I say
blood and beauty are identical twins
born of love and laid in a manger.
And to love is to live
and to live is to die
and to die is to love.

I have held a rose.
I have been pierced by thorns.

Truth has not one nature
but two.

* "For beauty is nothing other than the beginning of terror."

MADONNA WITHOUT CHILD

1 Samuel 1:1–28
For C. D. Weaver

Better here than in some alley dumpster

It's the old story
    you birth a child
        only to give him away to a world
            that doesn't know it doesn't care
How, you ask? Have you seen
    the dump I live in
        the Bitch I room with
            the Slick who markets me
                like a side of beef on a meathook
                —got me in this fix—
A fix for a fix that's my story
    I guess I'm sticking to it
So is this kid

Four months in I was too big for the johns—
    Slick said no man will pay hard cash
        for a basketball with legs
Told me about the nuns
    Word on the street was
    they'd take you in
        give you a slab of a cot
            feed you half-edible food
                —at least it's not smack and cigarettes—

if there's room
    if you can survive the shakes
I begged I screamed
    looked like I swallowed a beachball

I survived
Long enough to get here—
    "Labor and Delivery" they call it
        Ninth Ring of Hell more like—
Who knew Satan's crib would be this clean?
    "Is there anything you need, honey?" Hell yeah
        A hit of honey-in-the-vein
            sleep without this elephant on my spine
                Peace sweet peace
O God it was like passing a watermelon
    one of those heavy long ones my gramps used to grow
        in his garden back in Tennessee
            best part of a summer day
                cool wet juice running down my cheeks
                    pooling on the picnic tablecloth
I was happy there

But just now, when she puts him in my arms
    All wrinkly squally sloppy
        with the bloody water of creation
            pooling on the delivery room floor
mine and his all mixed and mingled
    and I think of watermelon juice
I am happy again

until they pry him from my hands
    "Best not to get too attached."
        "Lend him to the Lord."
           "The Lord will Provide."
The Lord Giveth and The Lord Taketh Away
    Maybe be the Name of the Lord

I can see visions of that boy
    speaking Truth (he didn't learn it from me)
        making kings (I never made him one)
           opening his veins (not like I open mine)
                saving a world that doesn't know it doesn't care
it needs saving

So better here than in some alley dumpster

Like the one that'll be behind me
    tomorrow night when I'm standing
        on my old corner and the old story starts again
Again.

MATINS, CHRISTMAS MORNING

O magnum mysterium . . .

—FOURTH RESPONSORY FOR MATINS ON CHRISTMAS DAY

Mystery needs no consecration.
It sighs in the wind,
crackles in the hoarfrost,
burrows earthworm tunnels in the loam,
eddies in the water where trout hold, unheard, unseen—
. . . et admirabile sacramentum . . .

I wake before the house,
stand on the back porch in the wintry air
of the not-yet-dawn of day.
Cold flash-freezes sleep within my brain.
The dog is attending to his urges,
aware, I imagine, that the brittle grass he sniffs
and the wisps exhalant from his nose
are pregnant with Mystery.
It waits to be born.
Or no—
it is already here, has always been here,
before we began these daily offices
of field and forage.
He knows.
He knows because he is Mystery.
He clothes Mystery in the soft swaddling of his fur.
. . .ut animalia viderunt . . .

Borrowed Question:
Why is this night different from all others?
Answer 1: It is the same as every other.
Answer 2: There has never been another like it.
Answer 3: It is the womb of a new creation.

Dawn breaks, a birthing mother.
Fluid light soaks the horizon.
Mystery is being born. Again.
Each morning is birth,
each evening is death,
  . . . dominum natum iacentem in praesepio . . .

Sanguine and pure,
Mystery pulses in the veins of creation,
coursing with the nourishment of life—
or spills, pouring out onto the land,
a death that does not die
but seeps between the living rocks
down to the light-starved caverns of creation,
an aquifer recharged by wonder,
a quickening at last
in the womb's dark heart.
It gestates there, in night-bound silence, waiting . . .
  *. . . O beata virgo, cuius viscera meruerunt portare dominum Iesum
Christum . . .*

The dog has finished his oblations.
I cinch my robe against the cold
and reach behind me for the doorknob.
Inside is warmth, and food, and she, asleep.

Why is this day different from all others?

It is no different.

There will never be another like it.

Mystery is born this day. Again.

. . . *Alleluia.*

THE WASP[1]

Mark 11:12–14
Monday

On a normal day a fig tree is just a fig tree.
Middle Eastern *Ficus carica*
grows wild where winters aren't so bone-deep cold
and summers linger long and hot and dry.
Blastophaga psenes—the female fig wasp—
bearing pollen from a distant tree,
crawls inside the seed pod, tearing off
her pollen-laden wings, the mortal price
of fertility. She lays her eggs
and dies. The eggs birth larvae, male and female,
who dance time's ancient dance there in the dark,
after which he dies, and she emerges
to pollinate another tree. Spring comes.
Without the sting there can be no sweetness.

This was, however, not a normal day.
That is, it was normal in every way—
the sun was climbing high above the hills,
the ancient sign of nascent summer nearing,
the dream of wasp and pollen, seed and fig—
a normal day it was . . . until he came by.
En route to other errands, he was hungry
but there were no figs. It was said

1. Originally published online at *Ecclesio.com*.

he cursed the tree. But tell me: was he not
a wasp to pierce the seed pod's tomb-like darkness,
and spread his wings and die and leave behind
an altogether different sort of pollen
that yields a sweeter sort of fig? Spring comes.
Without the sting there can be no sweetness.

JESUS' DREAM[1]

Mark 11:12–24
Tuesday night.

He listened while they yammered about the fig tree,
the money changers and the animal sellers.
It was apocalyptic talk, they said:
a fig tree cannot bear fruit out of season,
a temple cannot operate without
tradition, and surely mountains do not fly
into the sea. He closed his eyes and yawned.

They argued on. He fell asleep and dreamed
a little dream. No heaven-rending vision;
just ordinary faces in the crowd:
a child whose upstretched arms begged to be held,
a woman merely asking to be healed
a leper yearning only to be whole.
They did not ask so much. He saw each one

while dreaming of an ordinary world,
the slow, patient turning of day to night,
the whisper of a breeze to lift the heat,
the juicy, sweetmeat taste of figs in season.
He listened to their ordinary prayers
as though there was an altar in his heart
and he the priest. He smiled, and mountains flew.

---

1. Originally published online at *Ecclesio.com.*

SNOW, AND ASPERGILLUM[1]

10 January 2021 The Baptism of the Lord

Falling since morning
    a whiteness common elsewhere
    but rare enough in these climes
    covers sights all too common here

    and now the world is luminous
    look my neighbor says how clean
    like life's washed in bleach made pure.
I see
    the Styrofoam cup still lying in the gutter
    a lump indistinct and cosmetized like
    a lesion swollen just beneath the skin

    and dog feces and mud—blemishes
    chilled in ice but neither lanced or healed
    they wait tomorrow's sun to come to light.

Inside the sanctuary
    the celebrant speaks the words prescribed to say
    at the font and grasps the aspergillum
    dips and raises flings the droplets

    over child and parent gathered at the mercy seat
    who've gamely renounced evil and its ways—
    a promise they won't keep of course and can't.

1. Originally published online at *Reformed Journal.com*.

They know
    it's worked in deeper than the bone
    a faulty step on the rickety ladder
    of the double helix of creation

    but still the prayer perhaps more fervent now
    (however frail) that this sacred aerosol
    might scour clean what whiteness only masks.

It's all we have.
It's all we will ever have.

WE WHO ARE ALIVE: FOUR
ESCHATOLOGICAL HAIKU

1 Thessalonians 4:17; Mark 11:13

We who are alive
wait for fig trees to bear fruit.
Not yet time for figs.

Temples not torn down
wait still for their rebuilding.
Three days is not long.

No sign of rain, but
clouds of possibility
gather in the east.

Therefore encourage
one another with these words.
Soon the time for figs.

VESPERS

Ash Wednesday. An empty sanctuary, after the service.

This room is full of words
impatient for the joust
lances tucked firmly into armpits
steam-breathed stallions paw the earth
eager for the charge, the clash full tilt
that aims to unseat the metal-clad meaning
of another. Broken preachments
are strewn like autumn's dried-up leaves
across time's rutted lists, here where
hearts once pierced are left to bleed.

This room is full of prayers
helium balloons full of pretty piety.
Nuncios to an alien episcopacy,
decrees dispatched from haunts
of haunted yearning, jostle for a seat
in confessionals where no one slides
the latticed screen to listen. Inflated pleas,
encyclicals to minor more familiar gods,
rise on updrafts; they burst their *bullae*
and cascade like falling ashes to the floor.

This room is full of hymns
that swell and rise then crest and sink
on ocean waves, like frigates made of air
laden with the music of foreign passions

canticles mis-navigated from missals
in strange tongues, run aground in
these storm-racked nights. Broken melodies
crash on the rocks of our disenchantment;
they leave their fleckèd foam marooned
on deserted beaches of comfortable habit.

Outside this room, night is falling
and in the darkness Something
presses its Nose against the windowpane;
insistent, It interrupts the reverie
begging only to be let in
to light and hearth and quiet respite
from the loneliness. Whining,
It would share Its gentle healing Presence
tendered in Its cross-shaped sacrifice
if only It could come in from the cold.

TRANSITIONS

ALL IT TAKES

For Allen Pendarvis (1953–2018)

Tennessee creek at the bottom of the hill,
ankle deep at the waterline,
two young boys with a summer to kill;
and all it took was a little time.

Humid mornings, after a rain,
swollen current stained with clay;
wait 'til noon for the creek to drain
and the water to wash the stain away.

Crawdad pinchers can raise some blood;
learn to scoop them from behind
before they scurry beneath the mud.
All it takes is a little time.

Flip a rock in the bed of the creek,
see them scuttle for a hole to hide in;
like children playing hide-n-seek—
the only game we would never win.

Mothers call when it's time to go;
leave the water and begin the climb
up the hill and along the road.
All it takes is a little time.

So many rocks we never pried
up from the mud beneath the flow,
so many doors we never tried,
so many things we didn't know.

Up the hill and along the road—
you from your house and me from mine—
and never a thought how far we'd go.
All it took was a little time.

REFUGE

The barren earth where naught but sagebrush flowers,
The endless arc of azure sky above,
The dried-up wash, the creeping haze of hours—
These fixtures of our lives: just such is love.

But love is too a furious, fluid thing
Born of cloud and funneled into rivers,
Both nourishment of seed in hope of spring
And flood of grief that drowns what hope delivers.

Yet, betimes, the passing current slows,
Allows a moment's gentle introspection,
And gazing at the glassy surface shows
Our truest hearts in others' true reflection.

In life, in love, in drought and in deluge,
We are each other's most secure refuge.

THE TEACHER[1]

For David, on the occasion of his retirement

A quiet soul, forged in hardship's fires
yet full of stillness even if in pain,
he dwells in Beauty, and as thought requires

would have us see, would to the world make plain
how Beauty streams beneath this earthly crust,
how passing time cannot its flow constrain.

An aquifer of glory 'neath the dust
of mortal life, a vision few may see,
he would to our benighted eyes entrust

metaphors of Beauty (as must be)—
the crack of bat, the smell of new-oiled glove,
a golden dog off-leash and running free:

these are the passioned, pulsing heart of Love,
Beauty's other name, in which we share
as birthright, gift incarnate from above.

His quiet words, mere ripples in the air
are more than words alone; they are the Way
by which the Dark cedes place to Light made fair
and night yields up its power to dawning Day.

---

1. Originally published in the Fall 2023 edition of *Insights*, the faculty journal of Austin Presbyterian Theological Seminary.

PARTING: A VILLANELLE

For one whose laugh will be remembered

Let there be laughter at the journey's end
and grace, and little bits of ragged hope.
You will be well remembered here, my friend.

Away from daily sight, our vision bends
To gaze on ghostlier prospects, sadder tropes.
Still, let there be some laughter at the end.

We ask no more than time itself will lend,
nor seek now more than circumstance's scope,
but trust you to remembrance here, my friend.

You fly away and take to other winds,
while some here trace their tears down dreary slopes.
But give us laughter at the journey's end

As you are wont to do as treks begin.
Distance does not fray this mirthful rope,
and you will be remembered here, my friend.

So peace and joy and blessing now, and when
This life shall close its little zoetrope,
let there be laughter at the journey's end.
You will be well remembered here, my friend.

PARTING WORDS

For Ted

Here at time's edge, we seek those words that know
What time portends within its spinning gyre,
What path to other hearths, to other fires,
That passes on the flame you've sought to grow.
We would assume the task to fuel the glow
And nurture what your labors yet inspire
Until such time as time itself acquires
That holy place whence Fire itself must flow.

Yet only in that Fire will hearts perceive—
And not by human art but by divine—
The greatest treasure: not what we achieve
But what is giv'n: the long eternal line
That binds together hearts in heaven's weave
Where minutes measure not, nor words define.

BLUE-EYED SNAKE[1]

What in the world is a blue-eyed snake?
A sign that things are surely changing,
that what is old is sloughing off,
not yet replaced by something new.
It's hard to know just where you're going
when you can't see just where you are.

Snakes shed their skin. It's how things are.
It must be hard to be a snake:
about the time you get things going
your eyes grow dim and things start changing.
You have no choice: you face the new
blind as a bat. The first thing off

is eyelid skin. Before it's off
it turns opaque, and your eyes are
useless and blue. It's nothing new,
unless you don't know you're a snake,
can't understand why things are changing,
can't see which way the way the world is going.

I can't help wondering if what's going
on with us is not far off
from snakes whose skin is always changing.

1. First published in *The Presbyterian Outlook*

How vulnerable it seems we are
to fear of change. Like a snake
reflexively we hiss at new

threats perceived though unseen, new
phantoms in the fog, going
past in the dark. A shedding snake
will strike at you to warn you off.
I have a sense that's how we are
these days. Life is always changing;

new people keep arriving, changing
settled ways, demanding new
accommodations in how we are
used to speaking, used to going
about our days. Something's off,
we think, and learn to strike like snakes.

We're holed up like a blue-eyed snake.
The old skin's changing. Take it off.
We need new skin where we are going.

AN ARÊTE

is a knife-edge ridge at the mountain's crest, slicing
the atmosphere; clouds teeter at the precipice
before plunging—which way?—down
slopes past boulders bleeding out
into deep brown gullies on
the desert floor: either
before or afterward
east- or westward
to hope or to
despair.

is creation's monument to its own excellence.
At its apogee earth sublimates into sky.
In this rarefied realm there are
only ends, not middles,
truth or falsehood;
right, wrong;
good, evil;
yes or
no.

But stand beneath the ridge and watch
the cost of absolutes chip away at
the arête's fragile, faultless edge.
Sharp perfection refuses any
hint of negotiation with
rain and storm. So
the rock, friable,

fractures,
falls,

rolls
downslope,
splashing into
wadis where torrents
roil and buck. Grain by
grain, obdurate excellence
erodes away, toiling, tumbling
until all virtue, purity are at last
scrubbed clean, and rock and water come
to terms of compromise in the maybe of mud.

GHOSTS[1]

By blood and by choice, we make our ghosts; we haunt ourselves.
—DIANA GABALDON, *DRUMS OF AUTUMN*

You are not alone here.

The mirror cracks and shatters
In myriad tinkling falling slivers
That whisper like a Judas kiss.
A thousand eyes, framed by a thousand faces
Accuse, forgive, dissect and reassemble.
But the parts don't match, and symmetry
Is vanity's vision.
Did you think your secrets would survive this?

Your name, too, lies
Shattered among the shards.
It is not so much that you pretended
But that you trusted the pretending.
It is not so much that you dreamed
But that you thought you were worthy
of a dream.

No surprise, then, that this mirror broke,
But that it was one piece so long,
So many years allowing the impression
Of one face, one well-considered spirit,

1. Originally published online at *PoetryBreakfast.com*.

Serenity, solidity, self-control.
But behind the eyes, so many.
So very many.

Too shattered now for re-collection,
Too many razored reasons,
Too many jagged memories,
Cut deep the fingers given to repair.
The fissured faces speak with single voice;
From a thousand mouths, they tell
The truth:
No glue can mend the fragments of a shattered soul.

Mirrors are haunted houses.

CROSSROADS

Lord, I'm standin' at the crossroads, babe; I b'lieve I'm sinkin'
down.

—Robert Johnson

Somewhere down a Delta road, a cross
Stark and white against the greenleaf, raised
By some fervent Baptist, otherwise at loss
To understand why some souls are saved

And others damned. Robert Johnson, tale is told,
Met the devil at the crossroads south of Rosedale
And the devil wrapped his hand 'round Robert's soul
And squeezed 'til every song was a blues-y wail.

The one chord digs a hole where the soul should be;
The four's the soul's last struggle, though in vain.
The five's the height from which the soul can see
The one again, like a long black train

Arriving at the graveyard. Could we choose,
We all would sell our souls to sing the blues.

RISE

Rain and bone-deep cold.
I guess winter's finally come;
time for wandering is done,
or so I'm told.

But if I had a hawk's wings
I would sail above dark mountains,
I would drink from sacred fountains
and eat from tables laid with holy things.
And if I had an east wind
I would leave behind this lonely
and soar up high where only
hawks and angel wings have ever been.

Dogs out in the night—
noses at the door;
feel the cold air on their fur—
they want the light.

And if songs could erase
these failings that confound me,
I would gather them around me
like pups beneath a mother dog's embrace.
If I had the eloquence
to sing the angels' anthem—
poor advance on heaven's ransom—
perhaps this darkling world would make some sense.

Though wandering is done
wanderlust dies somewhat harder;
the heart's light reaches farther
than the setting sun.

So come with me, away—
pry open sun-blind eyes;
on some lyric thermal rise
above the clouded muse of yesterday.
Who knows what may avail
in Imagination's palace?
Perhaps some soothing solace
for a morrow full of yesterday's travail?

VOCATION

The mechanic works head underneath the hood
or sometimes on the floor, just below
the universal joint where the wear
and worry of the road reveals
its cost in fracture or in rust.

The mechanic knows the signs of systems
on the point of failure, that the brakes
won't make the excursion to the beach
or the transmission another month's
commute in familiar ruts.

The mechanic's fingers fondle curious tools
with esoteric names, like "tension wrench" or
"brake pad caliper"—names that retain
the aromas of psychology or science
beneath the smell of grease.

The mechanic works in silence, turning this,
adjusting that, and listening—always listening—
for the symphony of cylinders, the songs of belts
until the engine hums its tune and the parts play
in harmony of purpose.

The mechanic shuts the hood and wipes his hands,
stores the mystic symbols of the trade,
hands the keys to the owner, who pays and slips
behind the wheel and thinks he understands.
The mechanic knows.

His call is to repair, but not to drive.

AFTER THE STORM

Silence hovers like humidity
in the room. Prayers and sympathies
rise like steam in post-diluvian heat,
offerings to absent-minded gods.
He has little else to say or try or hope for.
But there is work, and so he rises too.

Gathers what the gale has left behind—
wedding photos, dancing hula-skirted
doll from Honolulu, Amtrak postcards
of snow-capped vistas in the Rocky Mountains,
the little Eiffel Tower made of pewter.
Each goes in the cardboard box he tries
but cannot muster strength to throw away.
For now, at least, the box is laid to rest
on the top shelf of the hallway closet
among the sprung umbrellas, widowed gloves,
detritus left by other, smaller storms.

In years to come, he will stumble over
pieces of remembrances once cherished,
but wind-torn, lost, and blown to god-knows-where
(Is there still a god who knows, or cares?)—
a candle-gilded dinner conversation
now come to ground in some neglected cornfield,
a shared purpling sunset repurposed as
a planter-box beside a front porch swing,
a pillowed smile before the lights go out

at night, now drained of warmth, mud-caked and drenched,
half sunk in standing water in a ditch.

He will stumble over them, and think
how strange they are and how alien,
will wonder were they ever really his,
and ask what sort of life would gather up
such random relics of aborted memory,
will rise, and turn, and slowly walk away.

FOR MARY OLIVER

Where you walk, I only look through windows.
Not because I fear the woods, the wind
that ever brushes clean the window sill
and sends the dry leaves roiling in the clouds,

but because there are the words to read
before they too roil away, and the time
to put on coat and hat seems like a treason.
And so your owl with unfurled fernlike wings

becomes in mind a strange transcendent angel—
oh, not a jovial, chubby, red-faced cherub,
but as you said, oblivion's memorandum.
Rilke knew: *Ein jeder Engel ist schrecklich.**

The darkened cottage opens to us all,
and all of us in time approach its door.
Yesterday you stepped across the threshold.
I peer through the window in my coat and hat.

*Every angel is terrifying.

PASSING THINGS

A generation goes, a generation comes, but the earth remains forever.

—ECCLESIASTES 1:4

The sunrise, against its will,
would choose the comfortable quilt of darkness
over ineluctable morning.
The earth turns.

Obvious things, mentioned for
the obviousness of things, the tiresome rote
of days. Yet beneath, something other.
Something new.

Swelling, pulsing, throbbing like
unsatisfied longing, hangover from a
future held politely to the lips
but not drunk.

Something is passing away—
disease, an order, a way of life, a dream—
We will all survive this, we are told.
Some, not all.

José Ameal survived
the Spanish Flu. Nineteen eighteen. He was four.

From his bed he peeked through drawn curtains
looked outside

to watch the souls passing by—
"so many dead"—on the streets of Luarca
in north Spain. Did he wonder if his
turn would come?

He lived to be imprisoned
by Franco, bury his wife in 'fifty-one,
marry another and live fifty
more good years.

Something is passing away.
We peek through drawn curtains at the procession
of souls. We wonder if today our
turn will come.

Tomorrow the sun will rise
reluctant, as though choosing its darkling quilt
over inevitable morning.
The earth turns.

WHEN I DIE

Use no pasty euphemisms: "He has passed,"
or "crossed to the other side," as though a sheep
slipped through some metaphysic fence for greener grass.

Restrain the pious "He's with God." No god may keep
what was not a god's to take and will not be.
Where gods demur to sow, they cannot claim to reap.

Stand to no overwrought or puff-stuffed eulogy.
Deeds, like fireflies, offer but the briefest gleaming;
their light a glimmer in the dark before they flee.

Decline as well the erudite discourse on meaning,
untangling some arcane apocalyptic thread
from the raveled skein, the knotted yarn of dreaming.

Brave the clean-shaved danger of the word: Dead.
At the end of every sentence, the Dark comes creeping . . .
and words, if living now, soon faint upon this bed.

Rather, raise a toast to love, though it be fleeting.
Sing rousing songs of courage, though the night draws close.
Then go your way to live, to pray, to sin, to sleeping.

Some say the dark bestows a blessing upon those
who sleep the trackless hours of the night. They wake
new-shaped, first fruits of new creation. Is it so?

Let it be so. For all must sleep, if not all wake.

DISGUISES

NWPH 12 April 1925—5 August 2021
Requiescat in pace

Sometimes death is a thief
who in dark of night gains entry
through the soul's unlocked windows
and steals that most precious of all treasure—
breath.
Or else a pickpocket in a surging crowd
who with deftest sleight of hand
snatches a wallet full of hope and expectation,
dissolves into the teeming throng, and
disappears.

Sometimes death is an enemy
whose ruthless forces, blades in sunlight glinting,
banners waving to declare the fight,
deny the living even one more day, one hour, of
life.
Or else a judge, benched in darkling robes
and somber, grim-faced and dispassionate,
pronouncing sentence upon one standing
in the well, innocent or guilty, who comes to
die.

But not today.

Today death is a faithful, trusted servant
late on his quotidian rounds, and hastening
to match his quota of souls who with overdue accounts
must wait, arms akimbo, foot tapping, for promised
rest.
Better still, today death is a friend, long lost
and long loved if also long delayed who, arriving,
taps quiet at the door to make us turn and,
with warming smiles, greet her as she enters, just in
time.

THE TREE AT THE EDGE OF THE WORLD[1]

A juniper tree grows at the edge of the world.
Bony-fingered roots claw at the face
of limestone, white-knuckled with the pain;
tenacious, they clutch the fragile hope
of strength to grip the ledge in howling wind,
of one more day to gaze into the void.

Gnarled and twisted limbs lean toward the void,
silent hands outstretched reach to the world.
What the tree gives up to scouring wind
it keeps in tortured lines etched on its face.
This stony perch the last outpost of hope,
last station in the dolorous path of pain.

What hand would plant you here to bear such pain,
such silent, lonely vigil in the void?
What mind create you testament to hope,
a stele at the frontier of the world?
What heart inscribe its suffering on your face?
What voice cry *Eli, Eli* to the wind?

No answer. The eternal moaning wind
soon or late will bring an end to pain,
will pry your grip from off the stony face
of life and send you spinning in the void.

1. Originally published in *The Presbyterian Outlook.*

Nothing so strong lives in this windswept world
As wind that wearies of the hope of hope.

And yet. You have been centuries of hope.
Half a thousand years lived in this wind
have shown you stubborn to the world,
inured to hardship, resilient in pain,
rooted in the rock before the void,
the suffering of joy writ on your face.

I have not the courage of that face
nor have I the reservoir of hope
to brave the emptiness, the void,
and cling to rocky ledges in the wind.
What I offer is my share of pain
To mingle with your joy before the world.

So shall we stand at edge of void to face
The world—the sun, the rocks—and dare to hope?
Who knows? The wind may yet bring joy in pain.

SIGHTINGS OF THE HOLY

Sightings of the Holy[1]

> In late September of 1973, I set out with GS [wildlife biologist George Schaller] on a journey to the Crystal Mountain, walking west under Annapurna and north along the Kali Gandaki River, then west and north again, around the Dhaulagiri peaks and across the Kanjiroba, two hundred and fifty miles or more to the Land of Dolpo, on the Tibetan Plateau.
>
> —Peter Matthiessen, *The Snow Leopard*

Peter Matthiessen's, *The Snow Leopard,* is a classic trekking tale, and like the best of such stories it relates a journey both physical and spiritual.[2] Matthiessen has two goals. The first is an audience with the Lama of Shey Gompa, the "Crystal Monastery" high in the Himalayas—an audience he hopes will steady the grief-wobbled gyroscope of his emotions in the wake of the death of his wife. The second is the sighting of a snow leopard, one of the most transcendent, beautiful, and elusive creatures on earth. Over the course of the book, the two goals slowly but inexorably merge.

In contrast to Matthiessen, Schaller hikes into the high mountains on a more mundane errand: to conduct a census of the bharal, or Himalayan blue sheep, the favored prey of the leopard. Schaller knows from long experience that seeing a snow leopard is more gift of grace than reward for labor; the animal is so stealthy and well-adapted to its environment that it could be hiding in the bush right

---

1. An earlier version of this essay first appeared in the Fall 2022 edition of *Insights,* the faculty journal of Austin Presbyterian Theological Seminary.

2. Peter Matthiessen, *The Snow Leopard.* New York: Penguin Books, 1978.

beside the trail and a passing observer never see it. But if the bharal are present in numbers, the leopard cannot be far away. Better to focus on sheep that do not resist being counted and trust that the leopard will reveal itself—or not—in its own good time. "Maybe it's better if there are some things we don't see," Schaller observes.

Still, the leopard hovers over the journey, a kind of spiritual presence lurking in the darkness at the edges of the sheep herd, always there but never quite visible, a symbol of beauty and of terror, twin signs of the presence of the Holy. In spite of all his watchfulness, Matthiessen never sees the ethereal creature. After three months in the high country, Matthiessen has to return home, leaving Schaller to finish the census. Two weeks after Matthiessen's departure, Schaller sees a snow leopard emerge from the under-brush just ahead of him on the trail.

Belden Lane writes, "The holy is seldom captured in the places where we seek it most."[3] I think he may be right. I have spent forty-two-plus years as a pastor, preacher, presbytery executive, and professor, wandering the high country of human experience, always keeping a weather eye out for some glimpse of transcendence. I am aware, however, that the more I have sought to capture and convey the Holy, the more it has eluded me. Despite all my eagerness for a vision of it, the Holy has appeared, if at all, only out of the corner of my eye or darting across my field of vision while I was focused on counting metaphorical sheep. The Holy, I think, runs and hides from frontal assault, ducks for cover like a trout under a mid-stream rock at the clumsy approach of an overeager angler.

When Matthiessen reaches the Crystal Monastery, he finds the doors shut and locked. The Lama of Shey whose wisdom he sought turns out to be not a saffron-robed sage enshrouded in a cloud of incense, but an arthritic old monk dressed in rags and curing a goatskin beside the road that winds through his moun-tain hamlet. "Form is emptiness," Matthiessen writes, quoting the Heart Sutra, "and emptiness is form."[4]

---

3. Belden C. Lane, *The Solace of Fierce Landscapes: Exploring Desert and Mountain Spirituality*. New York: Oxford Books, 1998. p. 80.

4. Peter Matthiessen, *The Snow Leopard*. p. 208.

My purpose in these pages is not to explain the Holy but to note mere glimpses of it. I offer here four sightings of the Holy, random sidelong glances at the Ultimate in the "empty" forms of poems and musings. The poems seem to me to cluster around the theme of the Incarnation, for Christians the definitive revelation of Beauty and the Holy. But it is not so much the content as the "emptiness" of the poetic form that interests me. I think of poems as open places, as invitations to the Holy to fill up the spaces between the words, should it choose to emerge from the underbrush. The power of poetry lies in the penetrating force of obliqueness, the apophatic dynamic of saying by *not* saying. Poetry can see the Holy, but only out of the corner of the eye.

I

Annunciation

Luke 1:26–38

Suppose it was not an angel,
but dust-motes floating in a shaft of light,
an idle breeze billowing the curtain,
whispering the wild and wordless wonder
of the ages.

Suppose it was not a message
from gods no one has ever claimed to see,
and from whom only madmen claim to hear
promises like these that strain the limits
of belief,

but merely a poor girl's fantasy
who had no sense of natural causation

and no better explanation near to hand
than godly violation of the sanctum
of her womb.

Tell me, could you blame her
for telling such a tale and, tale once told,
believing with a girl's ferocious power,
relying on the growing evidence
of her belly?

And if she believed it,
kept it within her heart, then why not we?
Why not the world—can it not make good use
of a god who yields up life in service
of the Holy?

Here am I, she said,
a statement less of certainty than hope.
And wondering if we could say as much,
we follow at a distance on the road
to Bethlehem.

Most exegesis of the Magnificat in Luke 1 focuses on Mary's apoc-
alyptic pronouncement of the downfall of the powerful and the
raising of the lowly. Mary is a prophetess of no mean proportion
in this way of thinking, the mother of the new creation. I don't
disagree. Still, I can't get out of my head the picture of a scared little
teenage girl, alone, pregnant, and terrified by an angel.

Rainer Maria Rilke insists that "Every angel is terrifying."[5]
In the same poem he also says, "Beauty is nothing other than the
beginning of terror." For Rilke, angels are symbols of transcendent
and overwhelming Beauty, something essential at the heart of

5. Rainer Maria Rilke, *The Duino Elegies*. "Elegy 1."

existence that cannot be comprehended or contained. The presence of an angel offers a glimpse of this Beauty, but it also reminds us that Beauty is forever beyond our reach and control. Beauty terrifies us with the vision of our finitude and mortality. To see Beauty is to see Death. I wonder if Mary knows the terror of the angels. I wonder if she senses in herself a wild rising anxiety as she contemplates what it means to be not merely a girl pregnant out of wedlock, but a draw card in the life-and-death poker game between Good and Evil. I picture her pacing the floor in Elizabeth's house, fear and desperation mounting, after the angel has delivered the "good news" and beat a path back into heaven.

Is desperation the first step on the path to the Holy? Is the first sign of the approach of the Holy that fierce hopelessness in the face of impossible circumstances that reduces your options to exactly one, no matter how fantastical and irrational and Hail-Mary-ish it may be? Does the Holy overwhelm scared young girls and render them willing to take any risk, brave any threat to follow where the Holy leads? I think hopelessness may be the purest form of hope, and hope another name for the Holy.

II

Not the Point

For Matt Gaventa

The star is not the point.
Nor is the manger nor the shepherds
nor the angelic caterwauling in the night.

The mother and father are not the point,
nor the cattle lowing while the world snores on,
nor—at the risk of heresy—the squalling newborn.

The Holy slips so softly into the world,
unnoticed in creation's warp and weft,
the hawks laser-eyed for signs of voles
don't see it.

    Nor you, from tallest steeple.
It makes nary a ripple in the water
nor transubstantiates the bread and cup.
You're bound to miss it. But know this:

if urgency of affairs or commands of kings
would hustle you away from purported holiness—
fear not. The star is not the point.

My friend Matt Gaventa, pastor of Austin's University Presbyterian Church, tells the story of waiting for hours in a long line at the Church of the Nativity in Bethlehem to see the ostensible birthplace of Jesus, only to be hustled along when he reached the spot by a guard whose principal concern was crowd control. I've been there. One hot August afternoon I waited in that same long line that snakes through the courtyard to the stooped little door, then down the stairs past the cave where, according to tradition, St. Jerome labored to translate Greek and Hebrew manuscripts into the Latin Vulgate, until it reaches the grotto where Mary supposedly laid the newborn Christ. Nothing about that place suggests to Western Protestant minds the birthplace of Jesus. The grotto—a niche in the wall the size of a manorial fireplace—is chock-a-block with lamps and censors and iconography that bespeak the devotions of centuries of Orthodox Christians. I found myself yearning for something simpler, something that to my Protestant eyes seemed to belong to the story of Jesus in the manger.

At last I saw it: bolted to the floor in the center of the grotto was a tarnished metal star, discolored from touches and tears of generations of pious pilgrims. It marked the spot, so they say, where the manger stood. This is it, I thought, the closest I will get to the physical locus of the Incarnation, the spot where the Holy penetrates the skin and gets into the bones of the world. I wanted to touch it, to linger there . . .

. . . but my rumination was disrupted by a guard urging me to move along, there's a large crowd behind you and the Church will only be open three more hours. So I moved, swept along by the mob in the current of the mundane, and the Holy evaporated into the vagaries of memory.

Back out on the street, in the midday sun, my senses cleared. I remember saying to myself, wait . . . did I just spend two hours to see a tin star screwed to the floor in the basement of a church? Is that all there is to the Holy?

Contemplating the decreasing likelihood that he and Schaller will spot a snow leopard, Matthiessen muses on being "spared the desolation of success, the doubt: 'Is this *really* what we came so far to see?'"[6]

I passed through the courtyard beside the sanctuary and looked across a busy Bethlehem street to a souvenir shop, apparently the place all the tourists went to decompress and memorialize their moment with the Incarnation. I went there, too. Oddly and suddenly, I found myself missing Pat back home in the US, so I bought her a necklace, a string of deep green malachite beads. Thirty-four years later, she still has it. Whenever I see it in her jewelry case, my mind's eye is filled again with the image of the grotto and the tarnished metal star. At the time, I thought I had been deprived of my encounter with the Holy that day. In retrospect, I'm not so sure.

III

Hagar's Prayer

Genesis 21:15–19

---

6. Peter Matthiessen, *The Snow Leopard,* p. 240.

When the water in the skin is gone . . .
gone too my hopes, my faith, my dreams,
my future, and not mine alone, but his,
squalling 'neath the wood, life just begun . . .
I turn away. Best not to watch the end.
Quiet, little one. Death draws near.

Hyenas haunt these wastes like ghosts, near
almost to touch. Their laughter, never gone,
mocks fate, curdles in my ears. The end
is in their snarling grins, not in my dreams.
A prayer for mercy, then, ere end's begun,
whispered not for my life, but for his.

Dreams! Dangerous to hope that his
life matters, that prayer could beckon near
some angel whose dark ministry, begun
on bleak nights in covenants long gone,
may yet haunt corners of the old man's dreams.
Angels begin what only death can end.

And yet I harbor hope that at the end
some angel will appear and with him, his
salvation, this infant of my dreams,
who nurtured at my breast yet draws me near
and bids my terrors, phantasms be gone
and limns a path to dawns not yet begun

but inkled in the darkness. Here begun
would hints and premonitions of the end
be loosed in time—though time is not yet gone—

and worlds reshaped, aligned with love, and his
the face to whom those worlds draw near.
I dare to hope, to pray, to sleep. To dream.

A mother has so little left but dreams
when birthing's over and hard life's begun.
But here's the truth: though dark of death be near
dreams yet endure and love withstands the end,
and gath'ring 'neath the wood they trust in his
embrace, spread wide, till dark of death is gone.

O Angel! Bide 'til dreams and ghosts are gone!
Bid lives begun in death at length be his.
For nearest dawn is darkness at the end.

Some children are born into privilege and promise. Most are born
into heartache and dead ends. The latter, it seems, was the infant
Ishmael's lot as he lay beneath the bush in the desert. The child was
the son of Abraham with a female servant, Hagar. The stories tell
us that Abraham's wife, Sarah, could not get pregnant and so "gave"
Hagar to Abraham to conceive for him a son and heir. Not long
after Hagar conceived, so also did Sarah. Hagar birthed Ishmael;
Sarah birthed Isaac. But Sarah began to see Ishmael as a threat
to Isaac, and so demanded of Abraham that he banish the child
and his mother from the camp, toss them out into the wilderness
where death would eventually overtake them. Abraham, ever the
dutiful husband, carried out the deed. The old man may have had
divine assurance that there was a future for Ishmael (the text says
as much), but the boy's mother Hagar knew nothing of it. The last
of her resources gone, she laid the child on death's altar and waited.
All she knew was the laughter of the hyenas haunting the edges of
the dark. All she could pray for was one of Rilke's angels to make
the end as quick as it could be.

I wonder if Mary prayed for an angel as she sat at the foot of the cross. She must have watched her dreams dying, just as Hagar bore witness to death of hers. Perhaps she prayed for the angel who announced the child's birth to ease his transition into death. She could not have expected the unexpectable: that the Holy is death, but also life. That the Holy is the place where dying dreams live on.

IV

The Magi Recall the Star

Matthew 2

Epiphanies always have consequences.
Apocalypses always require assembly.

A star. A distant pin-prick—maybe
    light from an ancient orb gone supernova?—
portends the end of something, and the birth
    of something new. But what? Or who?
Why should this punctuation in the dark
    become the instigation for the journey?

The journey. Set your foot to paths uncharted
    impelled to some uncertain destination,
ask inconvenient questions of those whose power
    disinclines them to acknowledge answers,
barter time from old, bloodthirsty fools
    who sit on queasy thrones and dread the star.

The star. It moves, yet night to night the same
    point of light in the aching windswept darkness,
the cold black emptiness of space.

Like you, it makes its own strange journey,
setting sail to catch the Holy's breath.
It finds its destination in those eyes.

Those eyes. The child sees you, and calls your name—
a name you had forgot, or did not know
you knew, a name whose riches, undeserved,
will cost you everything you have, and more.
He looks at you, and in his eyes you see
the rising and the setting of your hopes.

Your hopes. Leave them behind, these selves you carry
the journey long, like treasures of the heart;
return, then, empty-handed, knowing nothing
but the light behind the dark eyes of the child.
Be haunted by that light. It does not fade
even as the star returns to darkness.

Darkness falls. You are night-blind, and groping.
Go home a different way, if home at all.

Rare as they are, encounters with the Holy change everything.
They reverse the polarities of existence. They cost you everything,
and even everything is not enough. They drain you of yourself and
replace you with another Self you did not ask for and do not un-
derstand. They require you to die in order to live. "Yet not I who
live," writes Paul, who met the Holy on the Damascus Road, "but
Christ who lives in me."

Jesus, says Mark, met a demon-possessed man near Gerasa
in the Transjordan. As Jesus was exorcising them, the demons
"begged him earnestly not to send them out of the country." Why
do demons want to stay home? Do they crave domesticity, fear
the uncertainty of wandering and wildness? Are the comforts of

home antithetical to the coming of the Holy? And is that why those possessed by the Holy so often find themselves pilgrims and wanderers? From Cain to Abraham to the magi to Jesus to the desert fathers to Peter Matthiessen, they fling themselves out into ferocious landscapes to seek the Holy in places where life and death are inconsequential matters. Does the Holy drain away who you are so Something or Someone else can fill you instead, possess and mold you, make of you something you never intended to be? Does "home" cease to be home anymore, so that going home is but another journey into a far country?

❖ ❖ ❖

Annie Dillard quotes the philosopher Martin Buber: "The crisis of all primitive mankind comes with the discovery of the not-holy, the a-sacramental . . . " Dillard adds, "Now we are no longer primitive; now the whole world seems not-holy."[7] She is right, of course; the operational position of moderns is that the world of phenomena is readily explainable by available means. We have banished the Holy to the far country. And yet . . .

. . . that strange tingling in the back of my scalp tells me that Gerard Manley Hopkins was right, too, when he said that "the Holy Ghost over the bent/ World broods with warm breast and with ah! bright wings."[8] If so, then perhaps the Holy is more adept than we imagine at sneaking back from its exile. Perhaps it is not so far from us after all, lurking in the darkness at the edges of our experience.

When Peter Matthiessen at last meets the Lama of Shey, he is struck by how happy the old man is. The old man's legs are badly gnarled by arthritis; he will never leave the high country to venture into the outside world. Matthiessen wonders if the Lama is content with his confinement in isolation. "Indicating his twisted legs without a trace of self-pity or bitterness, as if they belonged to all of

7. Annie Dillard, *Teaching a Stone to Talk: Expeditions and Encounters.* New York: Harper, 1982, p.87.

8. Gerard Manley Hopkins, "God's Grandeur," in *Gerard Manley Hopkins: Poems and Prose*, W.H. Garner, ed. London: Penguin Books, 1985, p. 27.

us, he casts his arms wide to the sky and the snow mountains, the high sun and the dancing sheep, and cries, 'Of course I am happy here! It's wonderful! *Especially* when I have no choice!' "[9]

Jewish esoterica calls the interface between the engines of divine creativity and the physical realm of creation *Shekinah*, Presence. *Shekinah* is female, and she is the womb that gives birth to the world. I love that image. I love the idea that the Holy surrounds and suffuses us, sighs in the breeze and smiles in the sunset. I love the thought that we float in the amniotic fluid of the Holy. It is not so far away, I think, but peeks through here or there, beneath this bush or behind that rock or wrapped in bands of cloth and laid in a manger. The monastery doors are locked, but the Holy is on the loose. The Holy is along the roadside, a crippled old monk curing a goatskin. The Holy is a desperate young girl grasping for a way to explain her life. The Holy hovers in the sweat-soaked ambience of an overcrowded tourist attraction. Or breathes beneath a bush in the desert where hyenas laugh their ghostly laughs. Or whispers in the wind-swept darkness, after the stars are gone. Or . . .

9. Matthiessen, *The Snow Leopard*, p. 242.